```
CHILDREN NON-F
j
818.5402 B55

Bixenman, Judy
Dinosaur jokes
```

9000765856

D1804186

C
Children's Room
Mead Public Library
Sheboygan, Wisconsin

Borrowers are responsible for all library materials drawn on their cards and for all charges accruing on same.

DEMCO

DINOSAUR JOKES

Written and Compiled by
Judy Bixenman

Illustrated by
Viki Woodworth

Text copyright © 1991 by The Child's World, Inc.
All rights reserved. No part of this book may be
reproduced or utilized in any form or by any means
without written permission from the Publisher.
Printed in the United States of America.

Distributed to Schools and Libraries
in Canada by
SAUNDERS BOOK COMPANY
Box 308
Collingwood, Ontario, Canada 69Y3Z7 / (800) 461-9120

Library of Congress Cataloging-in-Publication Data
Bixenman, Judy.
Dinosaur jokes / written and compiled by Judy Bixenman; illustrated by Viki Woodworth.
p. cm.
Summary: A collection of jokes relating to dinosaurs.
Example: How did the dino feel after the steamroller ran over him?
Dino-sore.
ISBN 0-89565-728-7
1. Dinosauers—Juvenile humor.
[1. Dinosaurs—Wit and humor. 2. Jokes.]
I. Woodworth, Viki, ill.   II. Title.
PN6231.D65B59 1991
818'.5402–dc20   91-17079
                                     CIP / AC

DINOSAUR JOKES

Written and Compiled by
Judy Bixenman

Illustrated by
Viki Woodworth

How can you tell how much a dinosaur weighs?
By his scales.

What should you do when a dinosaur charges you?
Pay him.

Where was the dinosaur when the lights went out?
In the dark.

How much did the dentist charge for filling the dino's tooth?
Forty dollars for the filling and four hundred dollars for the chair.

When do dinosaurs have six eyes?
When there are three of them.

Why is a dino like a lemon?
Dino-sour.

What do dinos become when it rains?
Wet.

Why are dinosaurs so big?
So you can tell them from goldfish.

Why do dinos paint their toenails blue?
Hmm I don't know. Why?
So they can hide in a blueberry bush.
Don't be silly, I've never seen a dinosaur
in a blueberry bush.
See, it works.

How does a dinosaur get down from a tree?
He sits on a leaf and waits for the fall.

What's the worst part of having dinosaur for dinner?
You have to eat leftovers for weeks.

Why are dinosaurs healthier than dragons?
They don't smoke.

Why did the dinosaur cross the road?
Because the chicken got sick of the job and quit.

What kind of dinner could you make out of a Stegosaurus named Sam?
A Sam-burger.

If a dinosaur raises vegetables in dry weather, what does he raise in wet weather?
An umbrella.

First dinosaur: If April showers bring May flowers, what do May flowers bring?
Second dinosaur: Pilgrims.

What kind of a crew do scientists use to find dino bones?
A skeleton crew.

Where can you find dinosaur lumber?
In dino-saw mills.

What do you get if you cross a dinosaur with a parakeet?
A messy birdcage.

When does a dinosaur sound like a cashew?
When he sneezes.

If Daniel the Dinosaur had twelve bags of apples and he gave three to Sammy Stegasaurus and four to Timmy Pteradactyl, what would he have?
Two new friends.

**Dinosaurs are pretty tough
  they'll even eat a tree
But they act like the rest of us
  when they're stung by a bee.**

How can you tell a triceratops from spaghetti?
The triceratops doesn't slip through your fork.

How do you stop a charging dinosaur?
Take away his credit card.

What does a dinosaur have in common with a Christmas tree?
Neither one can play the tuba.

What kind of dino borrows Sarah's shirts?
Tries Sarah's tops (triceratops).

Why can't you find a store that sells dinosaur furs?
Because nobody will wait on them.

What do you get when you cross a Tryannosaurus Rex with an onion?
A dinosaur that cries a lot.

What's worse than a dinosaur in your closet?
Two dinosaurs in your closet.

The stewardess asked the dino if he'd like a menu.
"No," he said, "I'll just take the passenger list."

Why is a brontosaurus so slow to apologize?
It takes a long time for him to swallow
his pride.

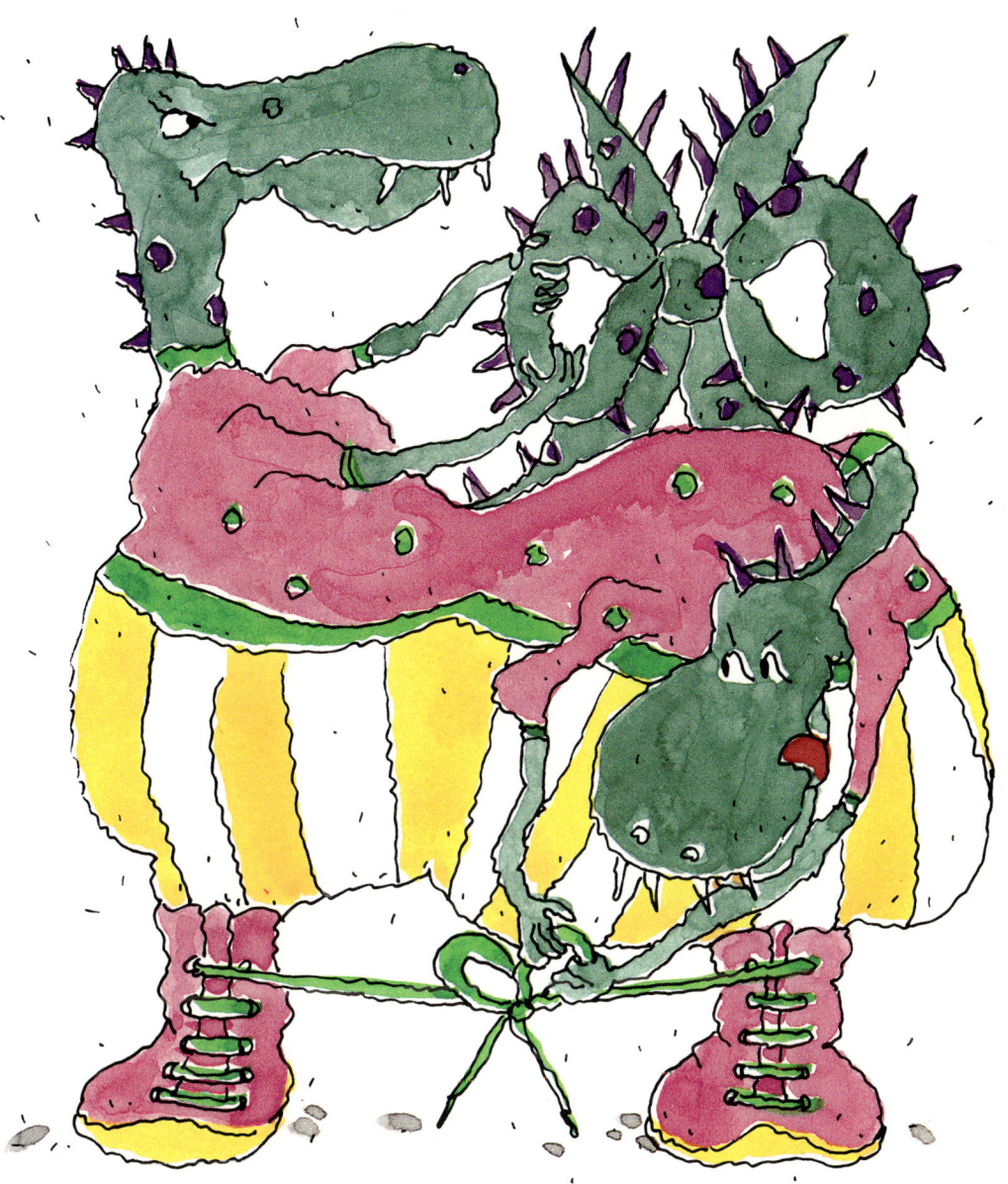

What do you say to a two-headed dinosaur?
Bye! Bye!

There once was a boy from Seattle
Who pretended he was in a battle
Then a big dinosaur
   stepped on his field of war,
And the boy was most quick to ske-daddle!

How do you take a dino for a walk?
On a hundred-foot leash.

What do you get when you cross a dinosaur with a box of toothpicks?
A giant porcupine.

When the allosaurus stepped on its tail, what did the iguana say?
Iguana get out of here.

What's the best thing to do if you find a gorgosaurus in your bed?
Sleep somewhere else.

How can you tell a mailbox from a dinosaur?

If you can't tell, I wouldn't trust you with my mail.

What do you call a dinosaur who lies down to wind his watch?
A sidewinder.

What's gigantic, elegant and furry?
A rich dinosaur with a mink coat.

Why did the dinosaur jump off the Empire State Building?
He wanted to make a big splash on Broadway.

What did the baby dino say when it saw the hunter coming?
Num-num!

Dinosaurs were very strange
   They never said a word.
And then they did the weirdest thing
   All of them disappeared.

What does an 800-pound dinamouse say to a cat?
Here, kitty, kitty, kitty.

Why can't Sammy Stegosaurus go swimming?
He can't get his swim trunks on over his scales.

What weighs two tons, twirls, and has sharp toes?
A dinosaur on ice skates.

Where does a dino sit?
Anywhere he wants!

Who taught the pteradactyls to fly?
Nobody, they just winged it.

What is scaly and blue and very big?
A stegosaurus holding his breath.

Where can you find dinosaurs today?
It depends on where you lost them.

What do you call a baby dinosaur?
A dino-mite.

What dinosaur is always breaking things?
Tyrannosaurus Rex.

**The two dinos danced by the light of
   the moon.
They whirled and they twirled to a
   beautiful tune.
The first said, "Please will you?"
   The second said. "Yes."
What a sight she became in her lace
   wedding dress.**

Mother dinosaur to baby:
   "What are you doing?"
Baby: I'm chasing that hunter around
the tree."
Mother: "How many times have I told you not
to play with your food?"

What do you call an 85-ton brachiosaurus?
Sir.

**How do you keep a dinosaur from going
through the eye of a needle?**
Tie a knot in its tail.

What do you get when you cross a skunk with a dinosaur?
I don't know, but it wouldn't have any problem getting a seat on the bus.

What did one dinosaur say to the second dinosaur?
Nothing. Dinosaurs can't talk.

Why do dinos wear green sneakers?
So they can hide in the grass.

Bobby Brontosaurus spent a long time at the doctor's office. What was his problem?
A dino-sore throat.

How did dinos get cavemen out of their caves for dinner?
Dino-mite.

How does a dinosaur catch a squirrel?
Sits in a tree and acts like a nut.

What do you do with a blue dinosaur?
Cheer him up.

What kind of dinos wear jewelry?
The finer dinos.

What do you get when you cross a dinosaur with a jar of peanut butter?
Either a dinosaur that sticks to the roof of your mouth or a jar of peanut butter with big feet.

How do you make a dinosaur squash?
Put it under a steamroller.

**There once was a dino named Doris
Whose family tree read like a thesaurus.
Her relatives names
Seemed long and insane
Till she translated all of them for us.**

Why do you think the dinosaur trips on his own footsteps?
Because the laces of his hightops are untied.

What do dinos have that nobody else has?
Baby dinos.

Why can't dinos be sweet?
Because they're a dino-sour.

What's huge, has four legs and a trunk?
A brontosaurus on vacation.

What's big, armored and has sixteen wheels?
A stegosaurus on roller skates.

What did the papa dino say when he saw the mama dino sitting on a pile of fruit?
Look at the orange marmalade.

What do they call the only dinosaur who arranges his tables and furniture very neatly?
The loan arranger.

What do you do if a dino charges into your bedroom?
Wake up.

Who got married at the museum's royal wedding?
Lady Di-nosaur and Bony Prince Charles.

Which dinosaurs slept most of the day?
The dino-snores.

What time would it be if five dinosaurs were chasing you?
Five to one.

Dinosaurs were bigger than
    a lot of us today.
They munched and crunched their way
    along and ate treetops for hay.

A dinosaur is something
    that you very seldom see
But if you should run into one
    the best advice is, "flee."

Tyrannosaurus Rex was fierce
    with big head and sharp teeth
But his front paws were so tiny
    he couldn't hold his meat.

Brontosaurus had a neck
    that stretched into the sky
But his bottom walked in water
    and his brain was mini-size.

Stegosaurus stomped along
    his scales clanging a song
But smaller prey would run away
    the music was all wrong!

Why doesn't the dino flap his wings when he flies?
Because dinos-soar.

What's the best way to catch a stegosaurus?
Lasso his horse.

How can you tell the difference between a dino and a marshmallow?
Marshmallow's sweet. Dino-sour.

Why couldn't dinosaurs run faster?
They hadn't invented tennis shoes yet.

Why do dinosaurs wear green hats?
So they can tiptoe across the pool table without being seen.

What do you get from a mixed-up lady dinosaur?
Scrambled eggs.